The Last Warriors

Face to Face with the Yanomamö

by Larry L. Baron 1989

Copyright 2015

Library of Congress Control Number: 2015900302

CreateSpace Independent Publishing Platform, North Charleston, SC

Contents

Acknowledgements

Thanks to Professor Robert Cameron for his encouragement and support.

Editor: Charles A. Black; Thank you for all of your hard professional work and for going above and beyond the average editor.

Thanks to Ralph Smith for guidance and advice.

Thanks to Jiang Hong for her support.

Cover Design: Adriana Hanganu
http://www.adipixdesign.com/

Trudy Tapenton: for helping me to further hewn my computer skills

This story is dedicated to the vanishing cultures of the world.

Dire Warnings

The turbulence of the plane jarred me awake. The constant droning of the air and engines drowned out the sounds of sleep from the surrounding passengers. As I stared out into the pitch black of the night sky I realized how alone I was. I realized how alone I would be as I embarked on this expedition.

If my plan came to fruition I would be travelling deep into the jungle, a lone westerner. Yes, I would have guides, natives who might be tempted to leave me for dead, and I would return to a life of ease with the money belt secured around my waist.

Lost in thought, gazing out at the endless sea of nothingness, I thought about my friends admonition.

"I've known you a long time. I know you're crazy, but I never thought you were a fool," Lightfoot's dire tone was like a wet blanket on my enthusiasm.

"I've been on trips like this before," I countered half-heartedly.

"Not like this you haven't! These tribes avoid men like you. The jungle is full of arrow ridden bodies that got too close to their villages,"

"I've got contacts that can get me there." The hesitation caused me to sound unconvincing.

"Ha! You've got contacts. They are going to get you in, but are they going to get you out? Why do you want to do this anyway? Are you trying to get yourself killed?"

"One hundred thirty-seven million dead!" I replied a little fiercely.

Lightfoot raised his brow, "What?"

"The American Indian Holocaust. The Europeans wiped out one hundred seventy five million Indians, ninety-five percent of the indigenous people in the Americas. Their ancestors go back thousands of years, and in less than two centuries they were exterminated."

"So what does that have to do with your trip?"

"You know I've visited indigenous tribes before, but this may be the last chance to see a completely un-acculturated warrior class tribe."

"Humph, a lot of good it will do you if you don't make it back to tell anyone about it."

Another jolt from the plane brought me back. I turned to see the guy sitting next to me open his eyes.

"I hate flying," he said smacking his lips.

We both reached down and managed to loosen the remnants of ice from our cups.

"Where are you headed?" he asked with a yawn.

"Manaus and you?"

"Rio. I'm going for a conference on trade. What's in Manaus?"

"I'm a trader."

"Really?" His interest piqued. "What do you trade in? I'm in textiles."

"Tribal art, artifacts, baskets, pottery, the more unique the better."

"Huh, sounds interesting. Do you have any trouble getting the real stuff or just knock offs made in the city?"

"If you know what you're looking for you can find it, but this time," I hesitated, "This time I'm going to travel up the

Amazonas to a remote tribe and see if I can get some rare items."

"You're pulling my leg, right?"

"No, why?"

He leaned close and looked me dead in the eye, "Look, I had a contact down here. We were thinking of bringing in some exotic cloth from a remote tribe. He went upriver to try to negotiate with them."

"And?" I asked, feeling my stomach churn slightly.

"And a few months later they gave up looking for him." He leaned back staring at me as silence hung in the air between us. After a few moments he added, "I don't understand why they are so hostile. We would have made it well worth their while."

"One hundred seventy five million reasons," I said flatly.

"What?"

"That's how many indigenous Indians were killed."

"Bull, there's no way. As dangerous as they are how could that happen?"

"Everyone thinks about the slaughters, of which there were plenty. But the Europeans were even more clever than that."

"How so?"

"The Indians had never been exposed to a variety of diseases; smallpox, the measles, even flus and the common cold. The westerners figured out quickly that by exposing the Indians to their sick and dead, they didn't need to waste a single bullet to kill them. Many tribes died out before they ever saw a white man. The lethal combination of diseases and war eventually wiped out about two thousand indigenous cultures."

"So what the heck makes you want to go in there if they may just kill you on sight?"

"I hope to see the Yanomamö, the last great warrior class Indian tribe. They've been able to preserve their culture for hundreds of years. I must get to them before missionaries infiltrate their homelands. Granted, geography and malaria have helped curtail intrusion, but their inner strength and their will to survive have propelled this very unique isolated tribe into the twentieth century. I have to go there before the ethnic cleansing begins."

"No offense, but good luck with that. I hope you don't get killed!"

"Me too."

Impenetrable Darkness

We retreated back into silence and the implications of our conversation weighed heavily on me. Was I heading into certain death? Was I a clever adventurer or a fool? Many hours had passed since we took off from the west Texas town of El Paso. The blanket of night was completely undisturbed. Lost in thought the ding of the seatbelt sign startled me slightly. Through the window off in the distance a tiny sparkle of light pierced the impenetrable darkness. It was the remote city of Manaus, the jungle capital of the Amazonas. Echoes from the bon voyage party crept inside my thoughts again. Exaggerated remarks from friends about the insatiable appetite of carnivorous fish, deadly poisoned arrows, chilling screams of blood-thirsty warriors, and vicious man-sized insects suddenly hinted at the imminent reality of danger. We were landing in an area where famous anthropologists immersed themselves into the most primitive Indian cultures in the world, often forfeiting their own lives. Was it worth it?

As a collector of authentic primitive artifacts, I knew that in order to get my hands on the most valuable museum-quality relics I had to take some risks. This trip, however, was the most dangerous one I had ever embarked on. February the 21st, 1989, marked the beginning of what would become the highlight of my thirty years in the field and my most difficult quest.

Apart from a money belt, my only other belongings were a backpack, a change of clothes; five shirts; a pair of hiking boots; a pair of tennis shoes; and two small flashlights. Unfortunately, I had forgotten to bring a raincoat. Apparently the geographical description *rain forest* hadn't registered while I was packing.

I had only done a cursory study on the Indian tribes I wanted to visit. Perhaps I inwardly thought it was too opportunistic of me to hope for to get the rare opportunity to encounter the Yanomamö. After all, the Brazilian government made it clear that foreigners were not welcome in restricted areas.

Like all my other expeditions, my plans for this trip were somewhat vague. Once I arrived in a particular country, I remained flexible. That way, if I was presented with a worthwhile opportunity, I was not held back by rigid schedules. This no-reservation trip to the Amazonas would ultimately turn out to be quite strange, exciting, exhausting, educational, introspective, and nearly lethal.

A Single Lead

I arrived in the jungle capitol of the state of the Amazonas, Manaus, at 3:00 a.m. Stepping off the plane, I was plunged into a steam bath. The Amazon climate, notorious for an unpleasant combination of heat and moisture, enveloped my body. I had to concentrate on breathing.

"God, I hope this taxi driver can take me to a room with air conditioning," I thought. With no reservations, we had to make three stops before finding a vacant room.

"Bon noite." I wished the cab driver goodbye, turned and walked inside the hotel. The room was slightly more than I wanted to pay, but the air conditioner was refreshing. Pretty girls were working the streets; their appearance advertised their skills and it was quite tempting. I slept until about 9 a.m. and went down to the lobby for some breakfast.

"Bon dia," I greeted the waiter. "Normally, I don't eat breakfast, but the smell of your freshly baked bread is too much to resist. And the fresh papaya and bananas are mouth-watering."

"Muito obrigado," I thanked him.

After I finished I walked around the old streets of Manaus. With no rain it was a beautiful day. It wasn't long before I found the Caja Bella do Flor (The House of the Hummingbird). What an appropriate name for an Amazon store.

I was filled with anxiety as I waited, but I knew the shop didn't open until 10 a.m. I didn't know the owner, but he was the only lead I had in Brazil. I flew all this way with just a single lead. "Would it pay off?" I wondered.

Finally I met, Richard Millnink, a medium-built man who was obviously well educated. He was an unusual American expatriate with a good sense of humor. We immediately hit it off. I couldn't believe my luck – things were off to a great start.

He showed me around his store which was full of beadwork, baskets, and eight-foot-long headdresses made of blue, red, and green McCaw feathers. They were collected from many present-day tribes living in the Amazonas. I was in Heaven. Unfamiliar with all of the different tribes, I was awe-struck by the incredible primitive artwork.

"Let's discuss business over lunch. You haven't experienced Brazil until you've tasted a famous delicacy from the Amazon River, the Pirarucu. It's a giant fish, with chewy sweet meat. It's one of the largest fresh water fish in the world. Here, this is a fingernail file made from this monster," Richard handed me the enormous scale.

"Wow. The scale almost covers the palm of my hand. I've never seen one this big."

"Some are much larger than the one you're holding. It takes a bit to cook, so let's take a walk while we wait."

"Sure," I said, looking forward to seeing some of Manaus before heading out to the back country.

"Manaus is an old city with a colorful history," Richard explained.

As we strolled down the streets, I tried to take in all the unfamiliar scents and bright scenes that flashed around us. The city was like a vibrant colorful maze of bustling sounds, rushing people, and pristine scenery. Walking past a fascinating building in a state of decay I paused, "What's that?" I asked.

"That's an ancient opera house."

"Do they still use it?"

"No, when Brazil dominated the rubber industry, Rubber Barons paid for the finest opera singers from Europe to come and perform here. Have you seen the movie Fitzcarraldo?"

"No."

"You've got to see it. If you do, you'll understand what Manaus used to be like."

"Can we look inside?"

"Sure. Why not?"

We opened the massive doors and squeezed in.

"Amazing!" I couldn't hide my excitement "I can almost hear the sounds and see the patrons sitting in the balconies. Truly remarkable. Right here, in the middle of the Amazonas, an archaeological shrine of days gone by," I said wide eyed.

"Those Rubber Barons had money to burn, literally. Filthy rich bastards. They felt the Amazon River was too dirty to wash their clothes in. So what do you think they did?"

"I have no Idea."

"They shipped their laundry to Lisbon to be washed."

"You've got be kidding. Lisbon as in Portugal?!"

"Yes. I kid you not."

"Paying singers to come perform for you is one thing, but sending their laundry to Europe?"

"In spite of that they were no fools; I'll tell you that much. The owners of the rubber plantations would befriend and entertain a potential rubber plantation supervisor, get him drunk, make sure he got laid, and coax him into signing a life-long contract while intoxicated. This self-made slave of the rich and powerful was forced to oversee a jungle rubber plantation for the rest of his life. His only human contact was with the Indian slaves he controlled until the day he died."

"They were slaves?"

"Technically, no. But, in reality that's what they were."

"What do you mean by that?"

"Well, if you never get out of debt to the company store, you're a slave. Time to eat." He ushered me back

The Flavors of Brazil

Sizzling over an open pit filled with red hot coals, the enormous fish looked delicious.

"This looks like an old ranch style Texas Bar-B-Q, but it sure doesn't smell like one," I proclaimed as the exotic smells filled my nose.

"Yeah, the sauces are classic Brazilian. It's covered with local fruits and vegetables to produce a flavor you've never experienced. That's the scent you're smelling."

"It's enough to make a man drool. I can already taste the fish." One bite of the Pirarucu, and I was hooked. With its firm and savory texture it was like nothing I had eaten before. The waiter brought over a couple of cervejas.

"What'd you think of Brazilian beer?"

"Delicious and refreshing for a hot day. Thanks for the fantastic meal."

"Let's just hope it's not your last supper," he chided me while toasting his beer.

Unlike the neurotic rush that we experienced while doing business in the States, Richard and I simply kicked back with a couple of beers for a few hours.

I thoroughly enjoyed our conversation. It wasn't every day that I came across someone so educated with the same eclectic interests as myself.

"I came to Brazil with nothing and started a warehouse. I managed to fill it with indigenous artifacts, and later opened a store in the center of Manaus," he explained.

"I admire your business skills, Richard, but I must say what I truly appreciate is how you're also preserving artifacts from vanishing cultures."

Richard was recognized internationally for his in-depth knowledge of Brazil's Indian population and their artifacts. It was obvious that he loved the natives and that he admired their work.

"Ready to see my warehouse?" Richard asked.

"I can't wait," I said with bated breath, imagining the cache of item that awaited me.

The structure resembled a bomb shelter and no one could tell there were priceless artifacts inside. I was somewhat disappointed by the appearance, judging the book by its cover, as people tend do to so often. Until he flung open the door

.

Don't Judge a Book by its Cover

I couldn't believe my eyes. There were thousands of artifacts stacked ten feet high—  beautifully preserved Indian art, hidden from the view of the general public. Intricately woven baskets. Yanomamö baskets. They were exactly as I had pictured them. Big, twenty inches or more in diameter and as deep as nineteen inches on average. Their black painted designs depicted the world as the tribes knew it. Highly stylized forms of circles, serpent shaped lines, or dots adorned the masterfully woven vessels.

"What does the black line mean?" I asked.

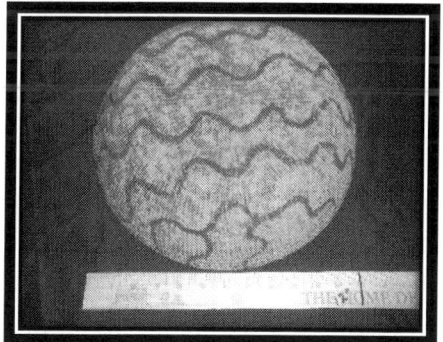

"That's a good question, but I'm afraid I don't know. All I know is that the symbols on their baskets are directly tied to their demonic belief systems. And their interpretation of the cosmos is almost a complete reverse to our own. Also, their cosmological world is not earth-centric; it is very complex."

"These baskets are amazing, Richard. How are they made?"

"Sounds simple, but what you are looking at took an unimaginable number of hours to make. Yanomamö women spend their childhood watching their mothers make baskets; it's an art passed from one generation to the next. First, she searches the surrounding jungle for the correct vine, cuts what she needs and takes it back to camp. Then she takes the mamuri vine in her teeth and tears the strands, one by one. After they are prepared, the strands are woven into the desired form. It's a long and tedious process. The women's teeth are worn out as a result of all of the tearing and pulling, eventually producing gruelingly painful abscesses, thereby making them more susceptible to early infection. They almost always die as a result."

I immediately ordered six thousand dollars' worth of the valuable native baskets. Richard gave me the opportunity to select the largest and best-preserved ones. I walked up and down the aisles of gorgeous creations, unable to make up my mind on which to choose. I wanted to buy them all, but my small business provided a limited budget. I couldn't believe my luck when he told me he shipped internationally.

The sun was beginning to set and the mosquitoes were starting to act up when we finally left the bunker. I returned to my hotel for a cool bath in anticipation of another exotic dinner.

Good vs Evil

Richard came to the hotel and we stepped out for a short walk before eating. "What are the Yanomomo like, now?" I asked him.

"They haven't changed much in the last hundred years. They are a fierce tribe and what is good in our minds is bad in theirs."

"What do you mean?"

"Exactly what I said. They reverse the meaning of good and evil. They think differently than us. But their culture is strong. They are a fearless, free, and proud people. They've had very little contact from the outside world."

"Richard......."

"Let's go have some turtle soup, grilled fish, and Brazilian style corn on the cob for dinner. I'm starving."

As we sat outside on a beautiful warm night under a full yellow moon, I had so many questions, but I decided to wait. "Last time I had turtle soup was when my dad and I camped out on the Clear Fork of the Brazos in Texas," I said as I looked with interest at the steaming bowl.

"Do you like it?" he asked me as I swallowed.

"Oh yes. It reminds me of some good times I had when I was a kid."

We washed our dinner down with a few Cuba Libres and continued talking, though not in depth, about Brazilian politics and the effect of the government and the missionaries on the rainforest. The direction of our conversation opened the door for more questions I had about the Yanomamö.

"Can you tell me a little more about the fierce people?"

"Well, it's getting a little late, but... They are demonic. The Shamans believe they are capable of conjuring little microscopic demons from rocks and leaves, storing the demons in their chests, and later causing a magical death. Shamans have immense powers and they are respected and feared by the tribe. Let's get some sleep; I have an important meeting tomorrow."

Back Channels

Two days later, while talking with Richard in his office about Brazil's Indian tribes, I made my request.

"I'm ready to go there."

"Go where?" he turned and stared at me.

"You know," I pressed on. "I'm ready to see the Yanomamö."

"You don't know what you're asking. It's dangerous. You can't go in the restricted area unless you get clearance from the Brazilian government or if you are working for them."

"I'm know, but I still want to go." I was hoping that the six thousand dollars' worth of baskets I had purchased would make him reconsider. He knew that I was willing to buy more.

"There may be a way. I hoped you'd change your mind," he paused giving me a penetrating stare. My heart stopped as he continued. "The FUNI will be leaving soon. The FUNI is a government agency that works with indigenous tribes in the Amazonas, and I think they are scheduled to deliver food in a Yanomamö area."

"That sounds great."

Slowly, he picked up the phone, made a call. He spoke briefly in Portuguese, and carefully lowered the phone down to his side. He looked at me and said, "They are leaving in three days. Are you sure you want to make this trip? This could be a one way ticket. I have to know now."

"Yes." I said as I firmly nodded.

Before leaving Richard's office, I stopped and looked back, "Do you have Yanomamö: *The Fierce People* by Napoleon Chagnon?"

"Got it right here on my bookshelf."

"Can I borrow it for two days?"

"Sure." As the door was closing, he called after me, "Good luck!"

I almost didn't believe it. I knew this was the chance of a lifetime. With hardly any time to prepare, I quickly scouted the streets of Manaus for essentials. However, unable to speak any Portuguese, I didn't have much luck.

There was no need to bring fresh water, I was told that there would be plenty of it on the boat. I knew I would need mosquito nets but I couldn't find any. The best I could manage to find was a few bottles of mosquito repellant and a thin plastic sheet just large enough to cover my body.

The next day Richard met me for lunch. "What's the trip like?" I asked.

"I honestly don't know. I've never been there. It's a damn hard trip, and you never know what will happen. The Yanamomo have the capability to go into a fit of rage in seconds and they're very aggressive. You need to be prepared for any kind of hostile action."

"You've lived here all of these years and have never been to a Yanomamö village?"

"Nope, never had the desire to take that much risk. They're very unpredictable. Haven't you seen pictures of their head bashings and chest poundings? Did you study their mythology? And, their vile temper is only outmatched by their pride. They see themselves as violent people. Not my idea of a pleasant trip."

"Yes, I'm familiar with their culture, but I still want to go."

"I hope I'm not losing a good customer," he joked. "You had better have read that entire book. Oh, and whatever you do don't tell anyone that you are an anthropologist. The government doesn't take kindly to anthropologists here, especially those who want to venture into remote territories."

"Got it!"

This was another time in my life when I realized that there were men who could always find a way around the rules. They just got things done swiftly and without any fuss. I felt that I could trust him, and intuition was the key to unauthorized travel in the back country.

Over the Rio Negro

A ten-dollar bribe got me a seat on a plane that looked like a World War II relic. Surprisingly the antique was in standing condition and it made regular trips into remote areas of the Amazon. It would take me deep into uncharted territory where few men had ever gone. That is of course if they could get it off the ground.

Hours passed as we sat on the runway in hundred degree weather paired with terrible humidity. I knew delays were common in third world countries and I had made my peace with that. But as time dragged on it begged the question. Would this broken down plane stay up in the air long enough to get me to my destination, or if my carcass and six cans of mosquito repellant would end up in the middle of the Mata with eleven other dead bodies? The tedious waiting was eroding my confidence. After losing an entire day with a splutter and some smoke, they finally got the engines started.

The sky was clear and the sound of the propellers was the only noise tearing through the silence. We were finally on our way. The plane left the ground with a lurch that did nothing to calm my nerves.

The area where the Brazilian government agents planned to take food and other supplies to the Indians was, as Richard suggested, restricted. There were ruthless miners trying to rob these protected lands. A veritable gold rush was taking place in certain Amazonas jungles and violent conflicts were constantly arising between the Indians and the gold rushers; tight restrictions on travelers into that jungle were rigorously enforced. If I were caught, I might end up with an extended vacation in a Brazilian jail.

I recalled seeing a *National Geographic Magazine* cover with an Amazon Indian chief on it. He boasted in an interview about killing nine gold miners with his bow and arrows. His life was cut short by a poisonous snake. No one was safe out in this unforgiving jungle.

After a while, we landed. I looked out of the window, but it was impossible to tell where we were. I could only guess that it was somewhere in the middle of the Mata. The runway was very narrow, surrounded by boundless nothingness. The only occupants were rivers and spectacular trees. There were no other signs of human habitation around us. Two passengers got off the plane, and immediately disappeared into the Mata.

As soon as they were gone the engines were started and the propellers roared to life. Speeding along the dirt runway we lifted off with a bounce as the plane groaned under the strain. All sense of time was lost flying over the Mata. It was a magical location of awe-inspiring beauty. When we finally spotted the next clear spot in the middle of the jungle, appearing amidst the permeating vegetation, it seemed eerie and unnatural. Only a short distance from Columbia, we could have thrown a rock across the border of Venezuela, and almost touched the Equator as we passed over three tributary rivers that fed into the Rio Negro: the Murie, the Curicuriari, and the Uaupes. I was spellbound. These were places I had only read or dreamt about.

I looked down and couldn't believe it. It was the small village of Sao Gabriel do Cachoeria. We were at the northern end of the Rio Negro, the biggest tributary to the Amazon River.

The bed of the Rio Negro hadn't changed its course to the Amazon for over 500,000 years. Its ancient igneous base consisted of pure unyielding granite.

Although beautiful, an unseen boulder was transformed into a kind of land mine for unsuspecting navigators. Most people who traveled by boat on the Rio Negro never did so at night. They stopped, anchored, and waited for the sun to rise up. Though they produced spectacular cascades year round, the rocks were extremely perilous for boats during the low water seasons.

Endangered prehistoric creatures like the Mata Mata turtle continued to exist in the Rio Negro and we were lucky enough to see a few of those majestic creatures. This river possessed a unique quality for travelers and its deviously tranquil waters were hypnotically inviting. Still, there were cautionary signs all around us: even the mosquitoes shunned these waters because of the unusual concentration of tannic acid. It was like The Rio Negro was a natural mosquito repellant. The acid was also the reason the river had a distinct brownish color.

Slashing our Way Through

As the small aircraft descended, an old sedan coasted up closely to the runway. Within minutes the scruffy driver had rushed me to my small room where I met my guide, Joal.

Joal spoke a tiny bit of Spanish, which was unusual for this place. He was about forty, and had worked in a Spanish restaurant in Manaus when he was young. His home was in one of the favelas on the outskirts of the city. These slums were inhabited by the poor, unfortunate and forgotten by society, one of the saddest places on Earth. With ram-shackled sheds, open sewage canals and diseases running rampant, they were the epitome of abject poverty. Most of the inhabitants were of Indian descent – the largest marginalized ethnicity in Brazil.

Our ability to communicate was limited, but Joal's friendly attitude and laid-back personality put me at ease for the first time since I left Manaus. I sensed I could trust him, and in the middle of nowhere, my instincts were all I could count on.

"Mañana, nosotros nos vamos," he said, "Tomorrow we go."

"Vale, bien," I replied.

Tomorrow seemed so far away. I wasn't sure I would be able to sleep at all that night. I watched them unload a forty-horse Johnson and thought it would take us up river quickly.

I walked down to the granite river bank eroded by eons of rushing water and relaxed as miniature cascades washed my feet. Small granite sand pebbles snuggled between my toes. The sun began to set, disappearing behind the almost invisible distant shore. Looking across the river, I could see one-hundred-fifty-foot tall trees running along the bank of the great river.

It was time to retire to my one-room hotel with no furniture and no windows. It dawned on me I was probably the only tourist it had ever seen as I closed the door behind me. The silence was permeating. This was my kind of travel.

I rolled out of the hammock at dawn, excited about our trip, but was met with Joal's somber expression as he informed me the forty-horse motor was "no bueno."

"What's next?" I thought. "Did I came all this way only to be stopped by some mechanical problems?"

The day dragged on while they made attempts to repair the motor. Before we knew it, nighttime arrived putting an end to their efforts. Disgruntled, I went back to my hammock.

The next day I woke up to find a new motor being loaded onto the thirty-foot flatbed truck. It was smaller than the original one, but it would have to do. We couldn't afford any more delays.

We were finally on the road and bouncing down the eighty kilometer rough dirt path, headed for the edge of a river.

Suddenly there was an unexpected stop. I asked in sign language, "Where's the river?"

Pointing to the huge trees a few feet from the truck, Joal signaled, "There."

The three men, who were accompanying us, jumped out of the truck and started slashing the vegetation with their machetes and axes. Finally, I could see the water but not the river. The undergrowth was thick and covered with hundreds of different kinds of species of plants. As they carved their way in, the water became a few inches deeper. After another fifteen minutes, the men had cut a hole long and wide enough to push the boat through the green wall.

We loaded the two thousand pounds of cargo onto the vessel. Despite what I had been told I never saw any fresh drinking water taken to the boat.

"Where's the drinking water?" I signed.

The Indian, squatting in the boat, picked up a tin cup, scooped up some river water, and handed it to me. At that moment, I knew I was in trouble.

Suddenly I felt uncertain about my decision. I wasn't a quitter, but the prospect of a fever brought on by and unknown water parasites or dysentery seemed unpleasant at best. Was I just being too squeamish and spoiled by the luxuries of city life? Surely, I could persevere and live like a true tribesman for a few days – these people had been doing it for centuries.

It was a no brainer. I had come too far to stop now.

Piercing Arrows

As we pushed through the tangled undergrowth, I was beginning to doubt an actual river lied ahead.

At one point we had to use an axe to cut through an eight-inch wide tree blocking our way. This route was obviously not used often. Finally, everything opened up into a wide clear space. We were entering a fairly large river that would send us on our way into Yanomamö territory. My excitement grew temporarily, washing away my fears.

The rest of the passengers on the twenty-three foot boat were unphased by the wild scenery around us. There were two Indian teachers contracted to work with the Yanomamö, a government outpost agent, two Indian assistants, Joal, and a Yanomamö shaman and his wife. All were capable of surviving in the jungle if need be.

I found it curious that the two young teachers, a man and his wife who spoke several languages, used a textbook written in the Yanomamö language. The Yanomamö didn't have a written language, as far as I knew. I had so many questions, but I didn't know if I could get an answer to any of them. I did discover, however, that this would be their second year to work with the Yanomamö. Upon a closer look they appeared to be missionaries translating the Bible into the native language.

Two questions kept running through my mind: were they attempting to preserve the language or were they associated with a missionary group that was attempting to assimilate the Yanomamö?

With the number of people on board combined with the two thousand pounds of food, the little craft was badly overloaded. I knew this was typical for third world countries, but it made me feel uncertain about whether we would reach our destination. Just trying to find a place to sit was an ordeal. This work boat was designed to navigate small rivers loaded with cargo but it was not designed to transport twice its legal limit.

We were all sitting there – as carefully as possible – an unusual mixture of people who wouldn't have met under ordinary circumstances. But we had one thing in common –

knowledge for the single most important law of the jungle: respect for those who were more experienced than yourself and that unseen dangers lurked everywhere. In a place where death could come in mere seconds, sticking with the herd and following a capable leader was the difference between ending up dead or making it out in one piece.

Piercing Arrows II

So many naive overzealous missionaries had gone into Yanomamö territory and come out floating in the river, face down, piranhas tearing at their flesh, their bodies pierced with arrows.

The jungle was a deviously perilous place, filled with numerous 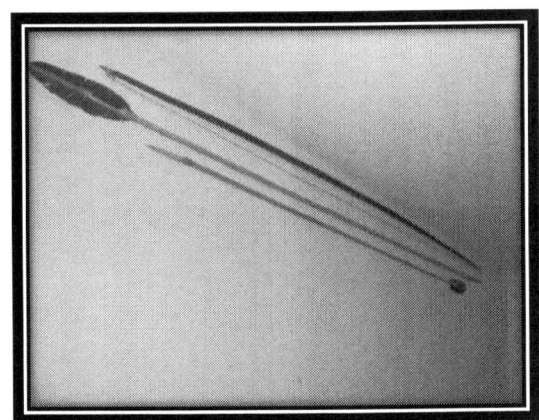 untold dangers and hidden threats. A simple cut or puncture wound was sufficient to catch a horrendous infection that could kill a grown man in a matter of days. The notorious Yanomamö arrows were fitted with poisoned tips. They were shot from bows six and a half foot long, made from the Palma Negro–the Black Palm. The wood was so hard that it was almost impossible to drive a nail through. The shaft of the arrows was cut from a sturdy grass which they grew close to their shabonos. I had only seen a few pictures of the large enclosed circular dwellings - all made from natural jungle materials that housed the entire community, sometimes up to a few hundred people under a single roof.

The warriors were known for their agility and brutality. They used three different types of arrowheads, a five-to-seven inch piece of bamboo-like material, sharpened on both ends and around the edges. This lethal 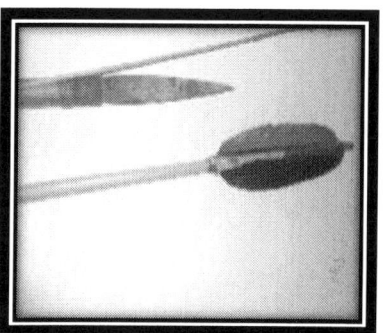 point was designed to come off the shaft when it entered an animal or a man. Once inside the flesh, the head turned and ripped blood vessels. It was an extremely efficient way to kill someone.

Another type of arrow was fitted with a slender piece of hardwood 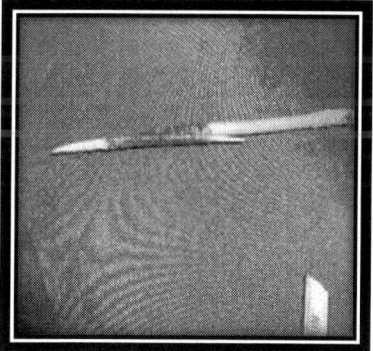 inserted into the shaft and hafted with a piece of a monkey's shinbone. The bone had been ground to a razor sharp concave point, producing a sharp barb on the opposite end. Once the barb entered the victim, it was almost impossible to extract. Usually reserved for fishing and bird hunting, the Yanomamö used both types in battle if need be. The warriors always carried a bow and one of each point types when they left camp. Sometimes they would even bring a thin pencil-shaped curare tipped arrow used to poison a target. It

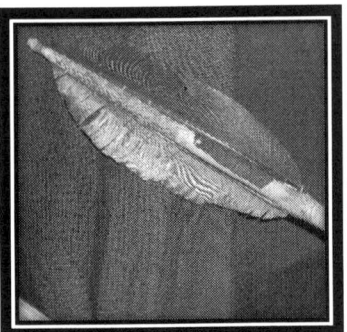

paralyzed the victim even if it barely pricked the skin. Yanomamö warriors used two feathers from a large black bird (Crax alector), a distant relative to American wild turkeys. Two feathers were artistically cut, slightly twirled, mounted to the back of the shaft, and carefully tied in place. The multiple rotation of hand movements meticulously meshed thread-like twine between each individual section of the spliced feather until one could barely see where a single strand stopped and another began. The two feathers were also twirled which caused the arrow to

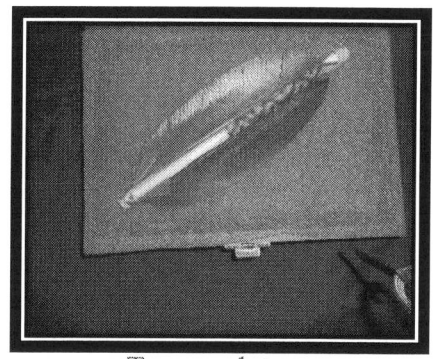

spin when released, increasing accuracy. To complete an arrow, a small wooden plug was placed in the nock in order to prevent splitting the grass upon release of the bow string. The final touches were the haftings of small but beautiful red and green parrot feathers on the distal ends of the black feathers. These artifacts reflected the pride, full splendor, and legacy of the vanishing culture of the Yanomamö.

Drinking Water?

Few people knew that most anthropologists weren't killed by Indians. They often died at the hands of their own guides who wanted to rob them. Sometimes an overwhelming sense of dread would wash over me, but I tried my best to chase away all the unnerving thoughts. I believed I could trust Joal and the teachers, although I was uncertain about the rest of the crew. I had enough money on me to retire the entire crew, at least by Brazilian standards, and I could swear at times I could see the flickering flame of greed in their eyes as the fire lit their faces after sunset.

The cargo to be delivered to the Yanomamö consisted of canned corn beef, large bags of rice, powdered milk from the U.S. (clearly marked not to be traded or sold, only given away), medicine, coffee, sugar, salt, soap, flashlights, batteries, perfumes, combs, shotguns with ammo, and one large gasoline fueled mechanical manioc grinder to be used for processing farina meal.

I thought I might be in luck when I saw some large plastic containers being loaded into the boat.

"Is that water?" I asked.

"No, gasoline," Joal replied.

February 27th began with some illuminating sunshine as we moved up the river against its moderate current. The small motor was straining to push our enormous load through the water. An emerald forest rose to enormous heights enveloping the craft. Howler monkeys screamed in the trees as we plunged past an explosion of butterflies. Their polychrome colors produced kaleidoscopic visions of nature's brilliant design. Lazy turtles clung onto half sunken logs while a fer-de-lance coiled on the bank ready for his next victim. Unseen, a multitude of species hid in the jungle foliage.

Thirsty, I leaned over the side of the boat and scooped up my first handful of river water. It was clear and tasty.

"Was it okay?" I wondered, but quickly reassured myself we were far from any civilization and the accompanying pollutants, "How bad can it be?"

I was uncertain about the prudence of this whole trip. But surrounded by all the beauty of this virgin land, a permeating feeling of gratitude was starting to take hold of me. And then it happened.

Torrential Rain

With little warning the entire sky seemed to be coming down on us. Rain. Cold, relentless rain. Torrential cascades that never abated during the entire day. The Indians grew anxious and it alarmed me; this was the first time that I ever saw them lose their cool. The men in the bow of our craft started throwing cups to the scattered passengers and screaming orders. Attempts were made to bail out the rainwater as everyone tried to squeeze their buckets and cups down through our huge cargo. We were trying to reach the bottom of the boat before the water level rose too high and we sank to the bottom of the river. I could see that the river water was about an inch from coming into the stern of our boat.

Bailing proved to be difficult because the cargo was so tightly packed. With all the water pouring in, the boat was becoming heavier by the second.

Even the Yanomamö shaman was shivering and shaking from the cold as he sat next to me and scooted under my thin plastic raincoat. The raincoat was the only protection I had. I bought it in Manaus but never considered buying a jacket or even a blanket - a mistake that would cost me dearly once the sun set. In the northern end of the Amazonas, the mountain region, temperatures dropped fast at night.

Then the unimaginable happened - in the middle of this unrelenting icy rain, the Yanomamö shaman stood up, raised his hands to the heavens. Then he began to wave his entire body dramatically, while chanting in a low voice. It was obvious to me that his was an act to manipulate the spirit world and take control of the elements.

Cold and Wet

Cold, tired, and soaked, we arrived at the first Yanomamö village shortly past noon. It was a brief stop intended only to drop off some goods. It was obvious that the Indians here had regular contact with the outside world. They seemed fairly acculturated, certainly much more than the Yanomamö we would encounter upriver.

We had picked up additional Indian passengers who squeezed tightly into the boat. It was customary in the back country to give a lift to others when possible. I had secured a small spot in the back corner of the craft and was curiously examining the new passengers. The pouring rain continued as we traversed four different rivers that proved to be sufficient highways through the jungle on this first day.

Exhausted, cold, and hungry, we finally made it to the first government outpost in the late evening. The dwelling was a wattle and daub structure, which had walls that were composed of horizontal and vertical wood slats filled with adobe-like mud. The mud closed the spaces in between the connecting supports. The structure was completed on the outside, but no work had been done on the inside. Two small wooden stools and some limited equipment were the only signs of potential habitation. This otherwise vacant building did include ties for our hammocks and a nice tin roof that sheltered us from the relentless rain. Most Americans would have considered it little more than a storage unit; however, after having been drenched all day, it looked like a four-star hotel to me.

I made an attempt to dry my clothes without any luck. They were soaked. We built another fire and ate canned food that night before collapsing from exhaustion into our hammocks. With heavy eyes I began drifting off and wondered why had we travelled so late to reach the camp? Then it occurred to me, the smaller motor could only push the heavily loaded boat so fast, and there was nowhere else to stay but here. Making camp just anywhere would have been too dangerous. We didn't have a choice.

The chattering monkeys and strange jungle sounds made for a strangely soothing lullaby. I quickly passed out in my hammock.

We had canned corned beef and sardines for breakfast washed down with black coffee. It was nearing seven am and the dense vegetation prevented even a single ray of sun from piercing its canopy.

A small Yanomamö village of only a few huts was within walking distance of our outpost, but the Indians were not there. I could see several ornate Yanomamö baskets I would have liked to trade for, but there was no one there to bargain with. Everyone had left for a ritual at another close-by village.

Not unlike the symbolic Catholic ritual of communion, the Yanomamö Indians literally ingested the body of their deceased. Upon a tribesman's death they would wrap the body in leaves and place it in the jungle for thirty to forty days where the natural elements deteriorated most of the flesh. The Yanomamö then retrieved the remains of the carcass and pulverized the bones into a powder. This powder was used as an ingredient to make a banana type soup. The warriors would eat the soup and in their minds, both body and spirit were consumed. This practice of endo-cannibalism is not uncommon in indigenous tribes.

Watching the Yanomamö shaman step back into the boat, I reflected on the tribal ritual and wondered if I would have a chance to witness such an act, hopefully as an observer and not a participant. As I pondered this, we prepared to leave.

A Gift from the Gods

We departed at dawn. The ice cold misty air cut me to the bone. My wet blue jeans felt like ice packs. That was another mistake I had made. I doubt I could have picked a more inappropriate piece of clothing for the jungle. I looked up at the clearing sky and back at the shaman who sat perfectly still, eyes closed, whispering unknown chants.

"Had the gods answered his prayers?" I wondered.

Brilliant sunshine illuminated the entire sky. This was the first sunshine I saw since departing from the States nine days ago. In a single day I went from a freezing cold bath to scorching heat. Naively I took the opportunity to change into my shorts in the hopes of enjoying the hot rays, but by the end of the day my failure to put on sunscreen had resulted in painful blisters over my legs, shoulders, and back. It was beginning to seem as though all elements were against me on this trip.

We finally stopped for a bathroom break. Fantastic. I worked my way from the back of the boat, climbing as fast as I could, desperately trying to get to the front. I made it; however, in order to get out of the boat and on to dry land, I would have to climb backwards over a giant tree that had collapsed on the bank of the river and get back to the vessel before they left me behind. By the time I got to the front, the Indians had relieved themselves and were already on board. No luck—I would have to hold it.

I was coming from a culture that valued privacy dearly and until this moment it was unthinkable to do my business in front of a group of people I had just met. But the jungle wasn't the place to be picky and protective of your personal space. Separating from the group was like an unfortunate game of Russian Roulette.

Joel told me a horror story about a tiny fish that could swim up the urethra, open up its tiny fins inside me and lock them in place when urinating in waist deep water. After that relieving yourself became impossible. It almost always required a surgical intervention and sometimes, God forbid, even amputation. And deep in the jungle it was clear if I found myself in such an unfortunate situation, I would have to be the one who had to do the cutting or die.

Just Around the Bend

I kept waiting for the next stop, but it never came. I put all my efforts into convincing myself that I had sweated out most of the fluids in my body during those tedious hours in the boat when the sun mercilessly beat down on me.

Each bend in the river brought forth spectacular views, and when we hugged the bank of the river, we could hear monkeys chattering in the canopy. Many trees like the Kapok reached over two hundred feet. Their trunks were gigantic. Flaring out at the base, they looked as if several different trees had fused together to form a unified platform for the huge trunks shooting up into the unseen blue sky. The land was shielded by a canopy of green. Their root systems surpassed the length of a football field. These Amazon forest giants were capable of growing to unbelievable heights in only thirty to forty years.

Without warning, we were hastily approaching fast running rapids and entering rocky shallows. It was becoming difficult for the motor to traverse these swiftly running currents. The vessel rounded the bend and came to a complete stop.

The Jagged Edge

Suddenly a waterfall blocked our path! The waterfall wasn't huge, but it was impassable. The jagged edge of the falls ruled out a frontal assent. Even if we tried lifting it straight over the falls, we would probably cut the bottom of the aluminum craft. Additionally, there were not enough men to lift the overloaded boat.

What could we do?

We secured the boat at the edge of the fall, pushed the vessel up against the bank, and unloaded the supplies. We then carried the entire cargo seventy-five yards up the treacherous incline, around the base of the mountain, and around the waterfall. Using hand-cut wooden rollers, we followed the same path and walked the boat to the upper end of the waterfall. Once it was secured to the bank, we reloaded the boat, and set off again through four hours of complete darkness. The crew, however, didn't need to see the river because they knew it by heart, and their keen senses guided our way.

They traversed the jungle by sound. In the darkness I quietly marveled at their abilities. It seemed to me the more 'civilized' we become the further from Mother Nature we get.

Hell-Bent

These guys were hell-bent on getting to our destination in two days. Our days started early and continued late into the night.

As we approached our camp, the waters started to calm. I heard a shotgun blast and ducked on an impulse; when I looked up, an Indian was pulling a four foot Cayman out of the river.

Getting close to midnight I was worn-out, but after finally being able to relieve myself I felt a little more comfortable. We had smoked and boiled crocodile meat for dinner. Cayman meat, white and firm, tasted excellent when boiled and when smoked over a freshly torn green stick grill, it was truly magnificent. I later used one of its three-inch-long teeth to make a necklace.

The Tukano Indians also managed to catch a number of different fish by netting them. The smoked fish made for a fine addition to our exquisite dinner. I continually admired the ability of the Indians, to make use of all of the available resources - something essential to our survival. In addition to their knowledge about the indigenous fauna, many of the natives had the ability to identify over a thousand plant species. In a place where so many poisonous species dwelled, this kind of knowledge was essential.

After the feast I was ready for bed, but I noticed no one else tying up their hammocks. "Why?" I wondered in alarm.

"Joal, aren't we staying here tonight?"

"No."

We regrouped, left the cargo in the boat, and headed inland in pitch-black darkness. Again I was reminded that this was not a tourist trip. They told us we had to walk about twenty minutes to another government outpost. But those twenty minutes stretched into more than an hour.

The walk was painful for me because of my sunburned legs. Each step I took felt as if my jeans were cutting into my thighs. My fatigue was overwhelming. My entire body felt drained of strength. It was clear you pay ten-fold for every mistake in the jungle.

We finally reached a bridge, which consisted simply of two long poles about five to seven inches in diameter. Everyone scampered across ahead of me. But as I attempted to precariously steady my uncoordinated body on the tight-rope structure, I couldn't keep my balance. My wet tight blue jeans were heavy and restricting; I almost plunged down into the darkness, but the thought of a Cayman, bush master, or boa constrictor silently waiting forced me to get a hold of myself and move forward slowly.

I flung off my heavy backpack in final desperation and motioned for an Indian to take my hand so that I could make my way across this stick bridge. We had to cross three more bridges before arriving at the distant outpost. It was now nearing two in the morning. 0

Completely exhausted, I had just enough strength for one last gleaming thought, "No wonder Richard never took this trip." Then my worn-out body collapsed in the hammock and I drifted off into a blissful haze of numbness.

Wattle and Daub

The structure was another incomplete wattle and daub outpost. It was only a mere skeleton of a dwelling. The wood slats had been erected, but no mud had been used to enclose the interior of the building. Except for the tin roof, this hovel afforded little protection. Also, as it was open at one end, a jaguar could easily come in unannounced in the dark of the night. There was not a scrap of furniture, but at that point in the journey, all I needed was some sleep and even the dirt floor would have been fine.

By now my main concern was not the possibility of losing all of my money, but the chance of simply disappearing in this remote region. No one would ever find me. With that final thought I passed out in my hammock while the mosquitoes feasted on any uncovered flesh. The next morning it was quite evident that setting out on a journey such as this without adequate protection, bordered on suicide.

"Get ready," said Joel. "We need to walk another fourteen kilometers to the Yanomamö shabono."

"Now?"

"We're leaving immediately"

I was completely exhausted, but I didn't have a choice. No one would have stayed back and waited for me to regain my strength.

Then, as if by some divine intervention, there was a glitch in the plan. For some unknown reason, we had to stay in camp for the day.

First, we needed to backtrack to our boat, where we met a large number of Yanomamö women. In their culture, women did most of the physical work, so this was not unusual.

With their painted black genipa lines and circles, nose plugs made from parrot feathers, lip insertion (which consisted of a variety of reeds), cheeks with extending six inch reeds, and adorned bare breasts these women of all ages seemed extremely happy. They loaded their burden baskets secured by means of a trump-line. Within minutes all of the cargo was gone, except for the guns and a few other presents for the Tusi—the

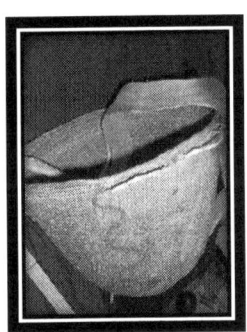

headman. The women disappeared into the jungle; we returned to base camp and waited for what seemed like an eternity.

A large section of land had been cleared all around the wattle and daub assembly. It was produced by using a slash-and-burn method - common in a tropical environment. The trees were cut down, laid fallow for a year, then burned, and the entire area was cultivated.

While admiring the cleared terrain, a cloud of tiny insects descended in droves and bored right into my pores. They were 'no se ums.' I couldn't see them, but these little blood suckers were devouring me alive. Each tiny gnat bite produced a blood spot inside the pore. And the worst part of it all was that the tiny wounds itched like crazy. It was impossible to keep yourself from scratching.

The Indians were also covered with insect bites, but seemed unconcerned. They calmly mashed and popped the nits right out of their pores. Soon I realized why. If those blood spots became infected, the infection would be much worse than the bite itself, especially in the jungle. While trying to emulate the Indians, I quickly ran back to my pack and grabbed the insect repellant. Needless to say, everyone was eager to get into my stock, which now amounted to three cans.

Overweight people were a rare sight in third world countries such as this one, so everyone was eyeing with curiosity the government employee in charge of the outpost; the man was at least four times the weight of an average Indian. And in typical fashion he was a happy, friendly person. I looked at him with envy. His obesity was an advantage in this relentless climate. Rivers of sweat flowed from his pores and drowned the invading insects upon contact. His entire body was coated with drowned no-see-ums, and there wasn't a single red spot on his soft, pink flesh.

The rest of the day passed in waiting. I was scorched during the day and shivering at night, stuck waiting.

"Por que não vamos?" I asked Joal. After all of this rushing into the early morning hours to get here no one was in a hurry to leave.

With our limited communication, he managed to explain to me that the headman of the village was absent. He was out with all of the young warriors hunting peccary, a South

American species of wild pigs. It wasn't safe for the crew to enter the shabono without him there.

This new delay was good news for my tired feet as I wasn't sure I could make a fourteen kilometer walk through the mountains anyway. My skin was solid red. I could almost hear it crinkle to the touch.

Extremely tired and with near third-degree sunburn, I would have an extra day to rest, recuperate, and rid myself of those pesky venomous parasites.

Since these miniature vampires loved the open fields of the slash-and-burn combined with the ever increasing heat from the sun, I wondered, "Why don't I walk over to the giant trees and get under the shade?" To my delight, it worked. The little stinkers didn't like the shade. I was relieved. The farther I walked, about seventy-five yards from camp, the fewer insects. I kept walking, enjoying the privacy, listening to the birds and monkeys in the trees. Then my path came to a stop.

Clear Cool Relief

Right in front of me was the most beautiful little stream that I had ever seen. It was inhabited by little fishes and a few other organisms, which indicated that this crystal clear water was not contaminated. I drank about a gallon of it. The stream was only wide enough for one person. I laid down and submerged my entire body. This slow moving creek caressed my sunburns and insect bites, easing my discomfort with every gentle movement. Needless to say, I made several trips to that beautiful creek throughout the day and each visit was more healing than the previous one.

Having a full day in camp, I had plenty of time to reflect on my first contact with the Yanomamö women and children. I was surprised to see the wad of tobacco inserted under their bottom lips. I had read they took a wild tobacco leaf, rolled it up, spat on it, and then rolled it in charcoal and dirt. They put it in their mouths just behind their lower lip similar to the American cowboys chewing tobacco; however, this Yanomamö method stretched out the lower lip not too appealing by Western standards.

The children were entranced by my sunburned body. They would sneak up behind me and put their fingers on my red skin, watch it turn white for a moment, and then back to red. To them, I was a walking enigma. They were having so much fun with this man who changed colors upon touch.

As they were laughing, running, and playing, I thought, "How could anyone think that these people were dangerous? They are just like other Indians I've seen."

The big surprise for the kids was when I took off my wet boots and revealed my porcelain white feet. They went wild, jumping up and down, laughing long and loud, as if my white feet were the funniest things they had ever seen.

Rested and ready for dinner, I was starved. Tongue-tingling smoked fish were sizzling on the grill. The meat of the fish was firm and chewy. Oranges, soaking in a cool creek, were readied for desert. Plantains, pulled right off the trees and thinly sliced, were laid out to be fried. An after dinner drink, something that I never expected, was a natural Amazon milk shake plant. Joal cut a hole, about the size of a quarter, in the top of a cantaloupe sized melon. Inserting a knife, he twisted it round and round several times, added a little river water, then shook it vigorously and handed it to me.

"This is delicious, muy sabroso, and it tastes just like a milkshake. Not quite as thick but just as creamy," I observed, pleasantly surprised.

After dinner I was ready for some sleep.

A Slash and Burn Nightmare

"Bom dia, Aberto, wake up!" screamed Joal. "Vamos!" I was sleeping heavily. Everyone was scurrying around and getting ready for the fourteen kilometer walk to the remote Yanomamö village. We traveled light since all our goods had already been taken to the village.

Relieved, I thought, "This is going to be easy." The jungle trail was cleared of brush and beaten down from foot traffic. I knew that I would be able to see a jaguar but not a fer-de-lance. For a brief moment my stress and fear abated, but it was short lived. We moved fast in the shade of hundred-foot tall trees.

"What the hell is this in front of us?" I peeked with curiosity.

Acres and acres of slash-and-burn had been prepared for horticulture. The trees had been cut and felled, but they were not dry enough to burn. The Indians scurried over them with no difficulty. Naturally, they were on their own turf. For me, this tangled mess of ten-foot-high vegetation was like a jungle obstacle course. It was all about balance. I had to struggle with stiff sun burned legs and sore muscles as I leaped from one branch to another.

Falling wasn't an option as I would have found myself impaled on one of the lower broken branches. Slipping and sliding, I climbed over the nearly impassable wooded obstacles. To the Indians, I seemed hysterical. They laughed and joked while running up to me and showing how easy it was for them to traverse this God-awful mess. My main concern now was being left behind. The prospect of being alone out here was daunting to say the least.

After the long grueling hike, a gigantic shabono, resting just below the mountain, appeared as if from nowhere. It had the classic oval shape, but its proportions were enormous in comparison to pictures I had seen. Tired, but overjoyed, I knew I would find some spectacular artifacts and learn more about the Yanomamö. This giant circular construct made from all-natural jungle materials housed a population of about 175 Indians, which was about two and a half times the size of other villages.

We learned that only eighty kilometers away was another large shabono, which had never been contacted by the outside world. Eighty kilometers was not a great distance for Yanomamö warriors; they frequently moved back and forth between the two villages.

When internal problems flared up in a Yanomamö village, one group always went its separate way and constructed a new shabono, giving the village a new name, planting a new garden, and forming new political alliances with other villages. These shabonos formed circles within the larger circle of the Yanomamö culture. When a shabono became infested with insects, it was burned and the villagers relocated.

Entering the shabono was like stepping into another world. I was so overcome with awe at seeing this perfectly preserved ancient culture, for a moment I forgot the deadly reality of the situation.

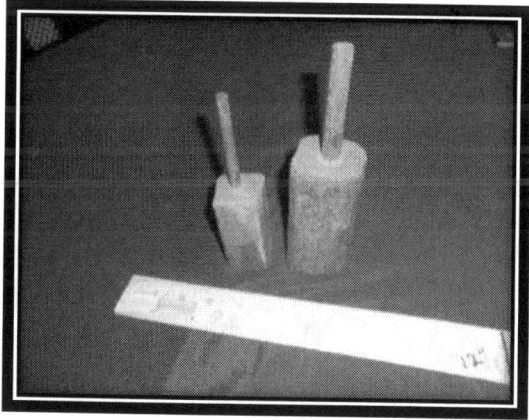

The building consisted of continuous individual unenclosed rectangular rooms joined together for families and extended families. It opened into an enormous hard-packed floor which provided a courtyard for its inhabitants – a structure reflecting the unity of its people.

Slowly, I surveyed the interior of the shabono eyeing the contents of each individual section and 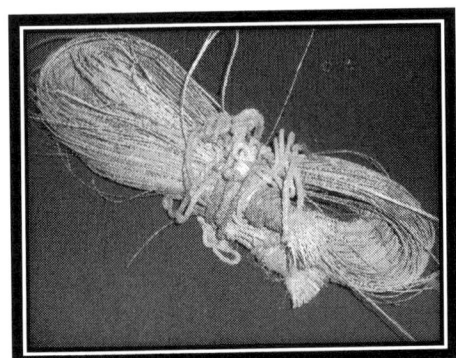 making a mental record of what I was seeing. Hanging from the ceiling were stunning burden baskets. Leaning against the wall or lying on the floor were twelve to eighteen inch gathering baskets. Magnificent six foot bows, slick and covered with shining patina, (the result of hundreds of hours of hunting and warfare), sat beside deadly painstakingly crafted arrows gently anchored in the rooftops. There were also drinking vessels, handcrafted from gourds and coconut shells draped over logs. A few government and missionary supplied single shot shotguns and hand carved shot gun shell loaders were leaning against the far wall; two types of hammocks were tied to supporting poles in each dwelling. Most were meticulously hand woven from a palm-like material while others were constructed of hand-spun kapok, a fiber gathered from a species of wild jungle cotton, making for a soft, plush bed. Delicious plantains, ready-to-eat dried meat, and dried fish hung from the interior of the dwelling. Heavy Brazil nut vessels used for storage were placed randomly throughout the dwelling. Tobacco quids that had been rolled in the dirt and fire ash, later to be chewed by men, women, and children, lay drying on the ground. Small wooden stools and hand-carved canoe paddles, fanning out broadly then tapering to a fine point at the bottom, rested against the walls. Sinister-looking demonic ebene-filled shaman's pipes, fashioned from long hollow reeds, were strategically positioned for the next ritual.

These long reed pipes were used by shamans to blow a hallucinatory drug, ebene, into the nostrils of another shaman. This action immediately caused an excruciating headache, glassy eyes, and long strands of mucus from the nostrils that strung to the ground. Rising from his squatting position, the recipient stood up and vomited before beginning a ritual that would transform his mind and body. He entered the demonic spirit world of the Yanomamö. I knew they believed a shaman's chanting could pull tiny demons attached to rocks and leaves from the edge of camp into his chest. They thought this powerful load could cause a magical death in even distant villages or anywhere else.

I was continuing to survey the shabono when suddenly a cold, still, deafening silence engulfed the surroundings.

The Demonic Shaman's Curse

A shaman stood in the middle of the circle, his hands reaching up towards the sky while his chanting seemed to reverberate from the walls.

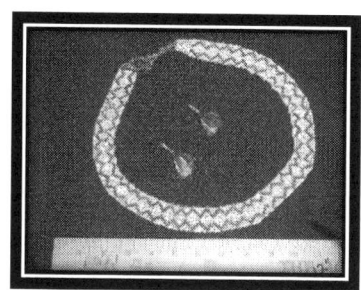

All eyes were fixed on this figure wearing only strings of parrot feathers that were dangling from each bicep. His penis was secured to his abdomen by a red, white, and blue beaded belt, a status belt, which was tied to the foreskin of his erect member. His

oblong face was streaked with red achote and his body was covered with serpent-shaped black lines. Dripping from his face were black zigzag designs and running down his body were tiny streams of black paint. He looked like the devil himself.

I knew that I was in the wrong place at the wrong time. I had been wandering around like a foolish tourist, caught up in the wonder of this pristine world. I knew better and my heart sank. I had added another novice mistake to the list on this expedition and worried it might have been the most deadly one of all.

In an effort to show respect I edged my way around the circle, and found a place to sit directly in front of his performance, but this was not a performance. It quickly became apparent to me that I had managed to make things worse, I sat in a sacred space. I thought about moving, but it was too late.

I was becoming the center attraction of the shaman's ceremony while he was screaming his chants, leaping forward then backwards in this blistering heat. Rivulets of black paint, fueled by his sweat, washed down his naked body. Drawing near me, he appeared completely unhinged. His relaxed scrotum allowed his testicles to drag on the ground as he squat-walked and jumped four or five feet from one direction to the other. Never losing his balance, this muscular shaman was incredibly strong and stimulated by drug-enhanced adrenalin. His demonic face was contorted and menacing. It was obvious that he was hallucinating to the point of sheer madness. Would he go into the classic Yanomamö rage? Closer and closer he moved with outstretched arms. He came within ten feet, then backed off to the center of the circle, chanting. Moving towards me again while squatting and jumping forward, he placed his hands within inches of my chest.

"What the hell was he doing?" I thought. I was ready to get out of there but I couldn't run. The Yanomamö had no respect for cowards. Besides, where would I had run to?

I was certain they would kill me if I showed fear. I tried to remain expressionless, but I was terrified. I sat there, frozen, following his every move intently. With hands and feet on the ground, he approached. Leaping on all fours with frog-like jumps, chanting loudly, he came closer and seemed to rise right out of the ground, only about twelve inches from my body. Then, in his frantic state, while both of his hands hovered over my shoulders, he continued to chant. After a few moments he backed off, returning to the center of the circle. I will never know what this shaman, in a place between the demonic world and the villagers, attempted to do to me or for me.

Did he put a curse on me or was this entire ritual enacted so they could justify killing me? I was an outsider. I meant nothing to them. I represented all of the hardships they had endured at the hands of the white men for hundreds of years.

A wave of relief washed over me. "God, I'm glad that is over with. Finally, I can take a deep breath and relax," I thought foolishly.

Knowing that these Indians could skillfully glide over fallen trees, sprint over slash-and-burn areas, tear through the jungle, all in a nimble, barefoot, agile and sure-footed manner, I didn't fool myself that I was a worthy match if circumstance put us against each other.

Attacked by a Mad-Man

While I sat in the sacred spot, another shaman, wearing a kapok penis belt and adorning massive scarification on the back of his head, moved towards me.

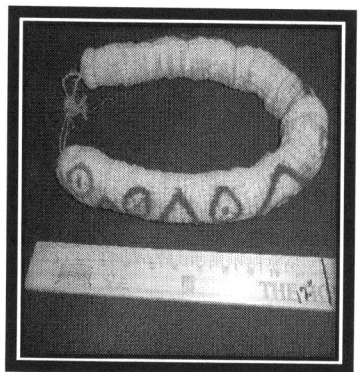

The deep scars on his head were status symbols. He had fought in many head bashing contests. He tripped over my foot, and pretended to fall forward. He simultaneously drew a small knife. Raising his arm over his shoulder, he turned and drove the knife down towards my throat. I reacted on an impulse.

Instinctively my right arm shot up to grab his wrist, blocking the blow. I quickly latched on with a vice-like grip using both of my hands.

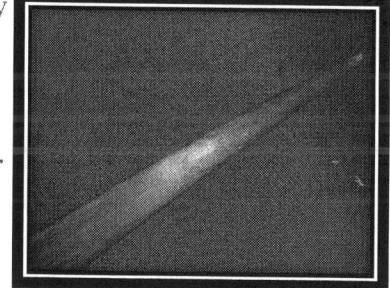

Now that I had a hold of him there was another big problem. What was I supposed to do with this evil looking SOB warrior class Indian in his own house who was trying to stab me?

I thought, "If I release my grip, he might kill me. If I don't, I will insult him, and he will kill me anyway."

Sweat ran from his stinking bald head. I was face-to-face with this devilish creature. Time seemed to have stopped. We were glaring at each other. Finally another shaman interfered. As he persuaded my attacker to calm down, I could feel a gradual release of pressure. I slowly mimicked his reaction without breaking eye contact. In this intense moment I knew a single sign of hesitation could prompt him to take my life.

Suddenly, as if nothing had happened, we both stood up and went our separate ways. I eased closely to a supporting pole and stood silently, trying to avoid showing any fear. For the rest of our stay there, I never my guard down again.

The Tusi had joined the younger warriors in their hunting expedition but came in earlier while the warriors were smoking the freshly killed peccary in the jungle. The headman was not an elected official, but he was recognized by the band as its leader. Like shamans, the headman had immense status. If he failed to lead, he could be removed immediately. I was relieved he had returned. Perhaps things would calm down.

Our crew had been invited to have some food in the Tusi's dwelling. His was the only hut that was completely enclosed. Like the shabono, it was constructed out of all-natural jungle plant material consisting mostly of post and palm leaves. Entering through an opening that served as a doorway, I understood the full scope of the honor bestowed upon us.

Simplistic, but much larger than I had imagined, this construction reminded me of some Zulu round-houses that I had seen. Its openness was inviting as we gathered around the center of the room and dined on boiled chicken and rice.

The Tusi exhibited the qualities of a leader. Like his peers, he was small but sinuous and physically strong. He radiated a kind of aura that reflected his inner strength and control. I felt at ease. I was sure that no more harm could befall us. I was wrong.

Cut off my Head?

In this subsistent independent hunting and horticultural system, monetary units had no use. We would be participating in a strict barter system. Even though the money I carried had no value to them, three young boys seemed to keep their eyes glued to the belt. Knowing that stealing was acceptable, I tightened it.

It was time to start the trading, and Indians were running around here and there in the courtyard. Cautiously, I began walking towards the center when another black-faced shaman bumped into me on purpose. He screamed something, and put his hand under his throat, making a slashing motion before he walked away. Killing was another thing that was acceptable in Yanomamö culture.

Stunned, I thought, "This one doesn't simply want to stab me; he wants to cut my head off!" I frantically searched for my guide, Joal. But he was nowhere to be found. I was lost in a sea of rotating Indians who were getting ready for the trading event. Joal, a Tukano Indian, didn't look much differently from the rest of them. I desperately screamed, "Joal! Joal! Joal!"

Walking up to me unnoticed, he put his hand on my shoulder for reassurance. This startled me and I jumped about six foot away. He just laughed.

I wanted to tell him what had happened, but there was no time. The trading was about to begin. Sticking closely to him, I eased into the center of the circle, sat down next to him, and tried not to stand out.

Joal was motioning to me to hand him trade items, as the Indians approached with their beautiful baskets and stunning bows and arrows. The Tusi was clearly in charge. Any challenges or disagreements during the trading were expertly handled by him. And, there were frequent tests.

When Joal pointed to the desired trade goods, I handed them to him. The trade items consisted of metal knives, bars of soap, trinkets, combs, and an array of other miscellaneous goods. Observing the bartering was fascinating. It was unlike any trading that I had ever experienced.

I was fairly sure that on more than one occasion the Tusi had to stop the trading and say, "Look at what we have received, two thousand pounds of goods, free of charge. These are our friends. They have come from a long distance to bring us these gifts, so let's make this trading event flow smoothly."

Of course, I couldn't understand the language, but in this highly charged trading arena, body language and facial expressions revealed with great precision what was being said. Much of the trading went smoothly, but there were occasions when grimaces revealed an unhappy warrior and occasional heated arguments would ensue. One warrior refused a trade for his bow and arrows and returned to his hut. The Tusi was a diplomat, yet he was firm and strong when the need arose. Without his presence, the event would have easily turned deadly. The Yanomamö simply may have opted to take our goods and refuse to exchange anything or just kill us. When the trading ended the Yanomamö seemed to be satisfied.

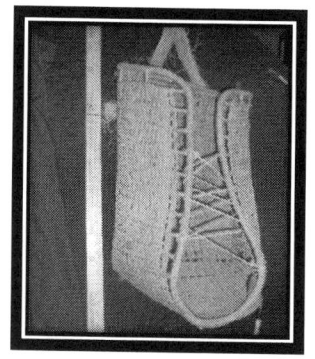

Suddenly young warriors proudly began trickling into the shabono carrying their freshly killed wild peccary. It was almost like a movie scene – one in which I was transported into another world, a surreal world of the primitive. Grasping their bows and arrows, they carried their smoked meat in strongly woven warrior's backpacks. It was obvious that the back packs had seen a lot of action. They were well-worn, tough, and beautifully hand-woven.

Skillfully wrapped in huge broad leaves, the smoked meat was delivered to their family units. I felt lucky that these young warriors were not in camp when I experienced the encounter with the older knife-slashing shaman. Though I was fairly strong, I did not think that I could have overpowered a young warrior. Had that happened, this story might have had a shorter ending.

Time to Go!

Watching one of the younger warriors unpack, I noticed some fresh tobacco leaves. Wanting to know what their tobacco tasted like, I motioned, using sign language, "Can I try some of your tobacco?" Another mistake. It was clear that he did not understand what I wanted, so I backed away. Stupidly, I didn't give up. As he was emerging from his hut, I made the attempt again. Agitated, he exhibited a hateful grimace, raised both arms, crunched his fingers, and screamed at me. That was enough. I turned my back on him and walked away, gambling that he would not jump me from behind.

Rejecting an invitation to a festival that night, the crew was busy assembling all of the artifacts that we had procured. I was relieved. After my encounter with the Yanomamö, I had experienced all of the anthropology I wanted on this trip. I, for one, was not interested in staying the night, and it was getting late. We had a long walk back to base camp. I was already physically and mentally exhausted when Joal handed me six Yanomamö bows to carry back to camp.

"No," I said. "I'm going to get this rear end out of here and that's all I'm going to take with me — nada mais."

I knew that when we hit the slash and burn area, I would have enough to deal with. Crossing the maze would be twice as difficult this time. Handing the Tusi my new buck knife, a folding hunter, I was not only hoping to promote goodwill, but also buy some life insurance. I demonstrated exactly how to open, close, and lock the blade. He appeared to be happy with my gift. With a silent jester, I signaled goodbye.

Darting in one direction and then another, our crew quickly assembled individual loads of artifacts and solicited several Yanomamö women to help carry this cargo to the base camp. I was the only one without a load to carry. This would be the only time I didn't help with the physical work the expedition demanded.

My only thought was to get out of there. I knew that Chagnon was almost killed several times by the Yanomamö.

He learned their language, spent over forty-four months with them, brought them valuable gifts, cured them of smallpox, hepatitis, and other diseases, and attempted to fend off the gold miners and missionaries. His entire career was devoted to helping the Yanomamö. And even his immeasurable contributions to the Yanomomo couldn't guarantee him safety.

Luckily, I found a twelve foot long sapling lying on the jungle floor before we reached the slash-and-burn area. It was small in diameter, but exceptionally strong and green from being recently cut. Without a doubt, this staff would help me traverse the sea of fallen trees and brush.

Slipping and sliding from one broken branch to another, it was impossible for me to keep up with these masters of the jungle. They were fifty yards ahead of me, then seventy.

"Un momento!!" I desperately screamed while stealing a backwards glance. "Is that black-faced demonic shaman behind me?" I worried to myself. "Un momento!" The emotional stress while trying to keep my cool and act unafraid contributed greatly to my fatigue. I was making some progress when my fanny belt broke loose and tumbled through a labyrinth of twilled wooden branches and rested flat on the jungle floor, ten feet below.

"Should I leave it?" I was way behind now.

One Wrong Step

"Un momento!" I screamed again, while lowering my body into the bowels of broken and pointed wooden spears at the bottom of the slash-and-burn maze. One missed-step and I would be trapped.

I managed to retrieve it, and thankfully it had only come unbuckled. Climbing back out, I remembered the three young Yanomamö boys who kept looking at it. They could have taken it. "Why didn't they?" I wondered. Perhaps I had just been lucky.

"Un momento por favor!" I yelled, as the group was now about a hundred yards in front of me. I was starting to panic. Getting lost in this jungle was a terrifying prospect or worse yet being left behind.

Keeping my balance was easier with the pole and I finally made it across the tangled mess of slash-and-burn. There was no time to rest. Thankfully they waited for me to catch up. The moment I arrived they moved out. I was ready to drop, but I had visions of having my head cut off, so I followed without a word. Once I realized that we were getting close to base camp I felt a small amount of relief.

I knew exactly what I intended to do. I planned to go to that stream, strip off my stinking clothes and jump into the cool clean water and relax. I could almost taste the water and feel it soothing my body. I was almost there, when, out of nowhere, a group of Yanomamö women scampered across the flimsy two pole bridge and headed right for me. They put their hands out in greeting. Since the Yanomamö do not actually shake hands, their hands barely skimmed mine. I couldn't rightly take off my clothes and fall into the cool water now. I would have to wait, but I didn't know that my afternoon plans would never live to see the light of day.

Vamonos! The River at Night

Stumbling into camp I was surprised by a sudden shout from Joal, "Vamonos! Vamonos!"

"Now? We just got here. Where are we going?" My god! It was only about thirty minutes from sundown. "What in the hell is going on?" I thought, alarmed.

I was dead tired, but I had no choice. There was no cargo lying around, and the crew was hustling to get their personal items together and leave. They were ready in minutes. Naturally, I was right behind them. I hadn't stopped since leaving the shabono. I had to gut it up and keep going or get left behind and perish.

Striding down the bank in almost a trot, I could see that the twenty-three foot boat was completely loaded with artifacts. I didn't realize that we had traded for that much material. It was a magnificent trade, but had it been equally satisfying for the Yanomamö? Of course, the reason we were in such a hurry was because of how unpredictable the Yanomamö were. They were notorious for sudden outbursts if the warriors who had a change of heart. Then there was the real possibility of attack from another tribe. At this moment I realized that I was traveling with professionals. They knew exactly what they were doing.

Fantastic! I'll just sit back and enjoy my trip down the river. After twenty minutes I was beginning to relax, then putt, putt, putt came irregular sounds as the motor was slowing down. "Terrific, something's wrong with the motor! Lord I hope they can fix it."

"No hay. Não mais gasolinea," said Joal quietly.

"What?" I thought. "What in the hell are these idiots talking about?" We had made this trip up river for two days straight, and now we were in the middle of nowhere and out of gas! I couldn't believe it. We had run out of gas in the middle of an Amazon River at night. Why? What was going on? I was on the verge of panic.

Out of Gasoline!

Then, it dawned on me. We were going down the river and didn't need a running motor. Without the sound of an outboard motor, no one would be able to detect our location. The possibility of an attack was slim. These Indians were not stupid. They had calculated, almost to a cup-full, the amount of gasoline that it would take in order to arrive at our destination, but not to return.

I silently motioned for them to hand me a paddle. The Indians in the boat had never seen a white man paddle like me. They were absolutely amazed.

"You're bad at walking, but you paddle like the devil is chasing you!" Joal laughed.

Little did he know I thought he was. Vigorously, I paddled until 1 a.m.

Searching the river bank for the remains of some Yanomamö leaf huts we had seen on our trip upriver was fruitless. It was too dark. We were having trouble finding a place to sleep.

Eventually we stopped at an old dilapidated branch and vine structure one of the crew spotted. As we pulled up to the bank, the Tukano Indians were raising a fishing net which they had dropped into the river. It was full of small fish which we smoked on a green stick grill and hungrily devoured. The blackness of the night kept me from seeing what I was eating, but whatever it was, it was delicious.

I found it amazing that anyone could find a natural structure in the pitch-black of night in the middle of the Amazon. After quickly recreating a partial roof structure, we tied our hammocks. I passed out immediately from the exhaustion. Seconds later my hammock slumped to the ground.

I was too tired to care. Shivering on the ground under my thin plastic raincoat, my only blanket, I began to experience nausea. I thought it was just stress. In the darkness of the night I was beginning to think the Yanomamö shaman had placed a curse on me.

Illusions of shamans and jaguars permeated my vivid dreams. I slept restlessly as the inner linings of my stomach continued to churn, but at least I slept, unaware that jungle visitors were silently making their way inside my backpack.

"Comida!" shouted Joal as the crew prepared a breakfast of canned corn beef.

I tried, but the serving just didn't taste right. The cans had been exposed to the Amazon's relentless heat. "It's gone bad," I grimaced with disgust.

"Não, obrigado. Tenho um pequeno problema com o meu estômago."

Downing eight or ten oranges, I attempted to still the rising pain in my gut. I topped off breakfast with four or five plantains, convinced that fruit might help.

Bugged in the Amazon

Hopping into the boat was easier now. It was completely full of artifacts, but this cargo was not nearly as heavy as the load that we transported up river. I moved back to the corner of the boat, reached into my backpack, but a tickling sensation caused me to immediately yank my hand out. A swarm of little black critters went flying into the river. My entire pack seemed to be moving as my new guests poured onto my lap.

Fear and disgust took a hold of me as I watched Joal quickly dumping hundreds of the little black bugs into the river. Then he bent over the boat, and lowered the infested pack into the water to wash it out. I looked up questioningly.

"Nada." He said. They were not harmful, but they very well could have been snakes or something else.

Without stopping, we kept paddling and paddling, I never slowed down all day. I was ready to get back to civilization.

Finally, after dark, we pulled into that first government outpost. Astonishingly, there was plenty of gasoline available.

Falling into my hammock, I passed out and dreamed of a demonic shaman. My dreams were becoming more vivid and menacing. I wondered what that could possibly mean.

We needed to travel upriver in order to traverse waterways that would take us to our final destination, back where we started.

This was our sixth day in the jungle, and everyone was ready to have a cup of java. Joal handed me a piece of red fruit with spines that I had never seen. I tasted it and spat it out as soon as my tongue made contact with this devilish morsel. The seeds were hot.

He chuckled. "Vamonos," he shouted, and we all jumped into the boat and continued up river.

I finally felt at ease for the first time in days. Anticipating an early arrival, things were looking good. The weather was on our side, and we had plenty of gas for the trip back. I was feeling fine, except for the pain in my stomach. I had no idea about what was going on inside my body. But the day was absolutely beautiful, and I was overjoyed to be leaving.

Arriving early was a welcome surprise since other days had extended well into the night or even the next morning. Trying to maneuver in the jungle at night was a real challenge. To our dismay, the truck which was to transport our cargo was nowhere to be found.

We waited for a short while and then decided to strip off and bathe in the clear, still waters of the river, clean up, and relax. The tranquility of lying in the cool water only lasted a few short minutes. A burst of thunder was followed by a huge raincloud which moved in without warning. We were drenched, and all of our clothes were soaked before we could even get out of the water.

What now? Without a truck and a torrential rain pouring on top of us things looked bleak. Joal grabbed me by the hand as we shuffled through the jungle in pitch black darkness before finding a small hut with a faint light escaping underneath its crooked door.

Knocking lightly, Joal spoke to its inhabitant through the door.

An Act of Kindness

A small, thin, muscular man with a leathered skin welcomed us into his one--room home. It was obvious that he was not from an isolated tribe, but his living standards reflected those of a poverty stricken, acculturated Indian. Even though the place was filthy and the cooking area was unsanitary, we jumped at an offer of boiled chicken and rice he had left over from his dinner. This was an example of the kind of compassion I would get the chance to experience many times during my numerous travels.

While the truck was arriving, I touched hands with him and thanked him in awkward Portuguese, "Muito Obrigado!" At midnight I was hanging my hammock in his little house. Sleep, I badly needed some sleep.

"Let's go! Vamos!" hollered Joal. The truck had arrived, and everyone in our crew plus about forty more people were making a run for the flatbed.

I rolled up my hammock, and followed the group; I paused, and when the owner of the hut was not looking, I dropped several cruzados on his table and ran for the truck as it eased its way out of the jungle.

There was no place to sit in the overloaded vehicle, so I ran around to the back and sprang on to the edge. I squeezed myself between two Indians. One of them was very sick. I don't know what was wrong with him, but he looked as if he were about to collapse. His eyes were glassy and he had a heavy cough. He seemed to be drained of any strength desperately trying to sit up on the back of our challenging transport.

Because there was no place to put my long arms, I placed one over his shoulders. Feeling a little strange about having my arm over his shoulder, I removed it. He then took my arm and pulled it back around him. Although I knew that he could not understand my language, I reassured him that we would get him to a doctor and that he would get well. He understood, and we became unlikely friends of circumstance. While bouncing on the back of the flatbed for eighty kilometers, I hoped my promise was not in vain.

Trading Never Stops

Trading never stops. Admiring my socks, my new friend made a feeble attempt to negotiate. While he pointed at them, I pointed at his beautiful parrot feather ear plugs. He shook his head, but 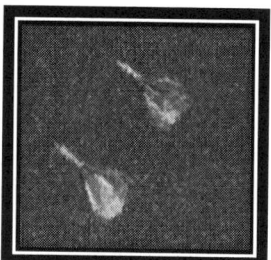 when we got off the truck, he handed me his earplugs, and I gave him my socks. He was quite content with the trade, but somehow I felt that I had cheated him, so I presented him with another pair. It was like seeing a kid at Christmas time. I have no idea what he wanted to do with the socks or if he lived long enough to enjoy them.

Back in Sao Gabriel do Cachoeira, I checked into a small single room with no air-conditioning that cost a mere three dollars a night. It had a real bed, which seemed like an otherworldly luxury after six nights in a hammock. In addition, it was possible to order a cold beer. This would now be my base camp for short trading excursions. I searched every fisherman's hut and attempted to buy artifacts and baskets. I also spent time simply strolling the scenic shore of the Upper Rio Negro. No other gringos were present. I was in a trader's heaven because the local fishermen traded goods with many unknown tribes in the surrounding jungle. I found unusually woven Maku Indian baskets, blow guns, beautiful hand carved canoe paddles, and an array of fantastic old artifacts. I couldn't stop for a moment. I kept moving, even during the heat of the day.

This was a mistake as I was about to find out. I was becoming dehydrated and was quickly losing weight, but what affected me the most was not just the work, it was the overwhelming heat and dehydration.

I was being eaten alive from the inside out.

A Spectacular Canoe

Seventeen and a half feet long! A spectacular Palma Negro tree trunk had been transformed into a work of art. Streamlined and pointed sharply on each end, the main body of the canoe was only about an inch thick, but was so hard that a nail couldn't be driven into it. Yet, it was light enough that it only required two warriors to transfer the vessel from one river to the next. I had already purchased two canoes, but they couldn't hold a candle to this one. It was obviously created by a skillful master's hand. I had to have it.

Catching the fisherman's attention, I motioned to him attempting to say, "Will you sell your canoe?"

We were about one mile down river from the village. He indicated that he did not want to sell, but I didn't give up. I had learned some Portuguese, including how to count. The numerical system was close to Spanish.

"Bon dia! Good day!" I screamed over the sounds of the swiftly running river. I didn't have a camera, but the image of this free man sitting in his perfect canoe, while the breathtaking rapids and isolated jungle surrounded us, is a precious moment in time I will never forget.

"Cem, Duzentos, Quatrocentos!" I kept offering more while he slowly paddled away. Luckily, he stopped, turned, and approached me. We struck a deal.

I motioned in sign language that I wanted to ride with him, and he allowed me to get in. That was another mistake. Most Indian canoes are not flat on the bottom; they are round. There was simply no way in hell that I could balance myself in the canoe. I almost rolled it several times before gesturing to the owner to take me to the bank.

He dropped me off and I followed along the shore. Rounding another bend in the river, we arrived simultaneously, dragged the vessel up a sloping bank, lifted it to our shoulders and carried it to the village. My cargo and this marvelous canoe would soon be on its way to Manaus, a six day trip down the Rio Negro.

"Onde está o avião ?" I asked. The plane was running three days late. I wondered if anything had happened?

Joal just shrugged his shoulders and said, " Possíveis problemas mecânicos."

I didn't care about the mechanical problems. I was getting awfully worried about my own plumbing. Spitting up blood became a daily ritual. What was happening to me? I had to get out of there and find a doctor.

Three more days passed and there was still no plane. Finally off in the distance the sound of a plane landing reached us from the field. Gathering my personal belongings, I was about to leave the hut when Joal said, "Não. Não é o avião certo. Este avião está indo para um campo diferente, no Manaus."

I sat back down in the hut. "Going to another village?" Shaded from the blistering sun, I began to exhibit signs of paranoia. "Why are they keeping me here? Do they want to prevent or shorten my stay in Manaus? What in the hell was going on?"

Two more days of trading without rest left me fatigued. I was making the most of my time in the village and accumulating more artifacts, but my energy was waning.

Coughing up more blood only contributed to my anxiety. "Why am I being held captive in this remote village?" Day nine was approaching, and I was determined to get on the next plane.

As the plane was landing, Joal said, "Não é bom, este avião está indo para outra cidade." According to Joal, this plane would not be going back to Manaus either. It was headed for another city.

While grabbing my backpack I silently thought, "Bullshit, I'm going to get on this plane. I don't give a damn where it is going!"

I've Got to Get Out of Here

Sprinting to the nearest taxi, I made hand signals requesting a ride to the ramshackle runway. After handing the driver a few cruzados, we took off.

The plane had been delayed due to mechanical problems. Someone informed me that I couldn't get on the plane because I was late. The pilot explained, "There are other passengers in other villages that have already signed up for the flight, and we're going to pick them up first." Then he stated, "Since you were late, you'll have to wait for the next flight out."

I said nothing. I waited. Mechanics continued to work on the problem. I sat there watching for one hour, two hours, three hours. Then, they all stopped. It was lunch time.

At about midway through the fifth hour, repairs had been made; however, it was now too late for the plane to fly to the other villages. The pilot was forced to return to Manaus. This was good news for me as it meant a seat became available.

I boarded the jungle hopper and squeezed in its only vacant seat. After a grueling ten hour flight, we landed, and I headed to find a place to rest.

"Bon noite," I said, greeting the desk clerk at the third class downtown hotel. It wasn't much, but at least the single room with its queen-size bed was clean and had soothing air conditioning. After the grueling jungle trip this was a relief. Cool, purified, bottled drinking water added to my delight. I was sure everything would be alright now. Exhausted, drained, dehydrated, and without an appetite I was ready for some rest. Still infested, I passed out.

Coughing up Blood

"A doctor. I've got to find a doctor," I frantically thought spitting up blood. I got dressed and rushed to the market. I was clinging to the hope that eating papaya would calm my stomach like it did in the jungle. I bought several and ate them all while standing on the street. They didn't help. A bad situation quickly turned worse when it became apparent I had lost even more weight and was becoming dehydrated by the hour. I had become a pathetic shadow of my former self.

Richard could help, but he was out of town. It was up to me to find a doctor. But where? I walked around, asking in Spanish for a doctor, rubbing my stomach in sign language, desperately seeking someone to help me but no one understood me. My Portuguese was insufficient to communicate my needs.

Finally, in the heat of the day, an older man wearing a 1970's hat came up to me. I could tell that he understood. He led me to a hole-in-the-wall private clinic around the corner of a downtown hardware store. Stepping into a line of about seventy people, I waited. When I finally got to see the doctor, we were both on the brink of utter exhaustion. With no verbal communication between the two of us, prescribing medicine for my problem would have been a gamble, but he did it anyway. It was the only option. Unfortunately I couldn't know that he had only prescribed a powerful painkiller, not medicine for the parasites that had taken up residency in my body. The pain subsided, but I continued to cough up blood.

During my stay in Manaus, I managed to assemble quite of a collection of miscellaneous artifacts from the local markets. The plan was to carry them with me on the plane back to the States in only five more days.

While working in the downtown area of Manaus, I spotted them. How could I have missed them? They stood out like a crippled duck in a pond–MISSIONARIES! Missionaries were walking down the street.

I ran up to them and eagerly asked, "Do you speak English?"

"Yes," replied a fairly nice looking woman. I could tell that they were in a hurry, so I explained quickly where I had traveled, how long that I had been in the jungle, I had drunk an enormous quantity of river water, and that I had been spitting up blood for several days.

Their saintly faces looked concerned. They knew the answer.

"What you have can kill you," she said.

"What do I have inside my stomach?" I pleaded.

"Giardia. They are tiny parasites that suck the blood out of your stomach until you die."

I froze – after everything I had been through instead of a crazed shaman, a microscopic parasite might kill me. She found a piece of paper in her purse and wrote down a single word, handing it to me, "This medicine will kill the parasites. Go to the nearest pharmacy and buy it right now!" she warned me.

In Desperate Need of a Doctor

In a matter of minutes, I bought my medicine without having to go through a battery of bureaucratic doctors and numerous consultations. I thought, "time, time was all I needed now."

Another two days passed. The medicine was working; however, I had made another mistake. Prior to meeting the missionaries, I had become desperate. Since I couldn't find a doctor, I attempted to help myself by taking various medicines for my stomach. At one point, I thought that I might have had hepatitis. Guessing that hepatitis might be the sole cause of my growing illness, I took an entire box of pills. Although I didn't take them all at once, the doses didn't come too far apart. I had probably taken enough non-prescription medicines to kill an elephant. Now, because of the missionaries, I was finally on the road to recovery and could prepare for my trip home.

Lying on my one room floor was a very large assortment of blowguns, arrows, and other ethnographic artifacts. I had to get this stuff packed. The plane was to leave for the States in only a few hours. Hundreds of items. All had to have a *Made in Brazil* tag fitted on them. It was the law. If I had any chance of passing through U.S. Customs, the tags had to be attached. It was now 7 p.m., and all of the stores that made tags were closed, and Richard was still gone.

"Villiam," I asked, "Do you know where I can get these tags?" Villiam was an acculturated Tukano Indian who had been converted by Christians. He now assumed the role of an indigenous Baptist preacher. He was very helpful when it came to packing; however, he was unable to find the labels I needed. After everything I went through to acquire these items I faced the prospect of having to leave them behind.

Completely exhausted, I was forced to lie down on the bed often. My head just didn't feel right, and I was having trouble focusing. The room seemed to be moving around. I kept telling myself, "Pull yourself together. You MUST get to the plane with this cargo." I couldn't rest.

I had no time to rest.

Finally it dawned on me! The hotel clerk. Maybe I could pay her to type "Made in Brazil" on hundreds of little labels. I scurried downstairs to the clerk's desk. A very nice, shy young lady was in charge. Attempting to communicate my need to her, with pictures and symbols I laboriously scribbled on a piece of paper. She went right to work. In a short time Villiam and I were provided with all of the necessary labels.

"Muito obrigado. Thank yo," I said when she finished. Then I handed her much more than the required hourly wage. She was overjoyed.

The tedious task of sticking each artifact with an Elmer's glue label dragged on for hours. We hadn't finished when Villiam had to attend a church function.

"Are you coming back?"

"In one hour," Villiam replied.

I collapsed on the bed, starting to get somewhat delirious, and passed out for about fifteen minutes. Awakening, I looked up at the ceiling which was moving in a blur.

Alone and scared, I looked into the hotel mirror and said, "Mind over matter. Go! Leave me," and then I started praying, "In the name of the Father, the Son, and the Holy Ghost, just get me on that plane. That is all I ask of you." There are no atheists in fox holes, including me, and I was in a fox hole.

I have always had a personal relationship with God in a different way from those who participated in organized religion. To me, God was simply a metaphor, a word used to feebly attempt to define the great mystery, a universal power recognized by all cultures worldwide; yet here I was, calling on the Judeo-Christian god, begging for help.

"In the name of the Father, the Son, and the Holy Ghost, cast off this awful veil which lingers on my body and soul."

Amazingly, using these words, I cleared up completely, body and mind. I could focus and was no longer exhausted. Was there an intervention of a higher power? Not being a church goer, I realized something. Spirituality did, in fact, transcend religion. If a label were required to describe my spirituality, probably Pantheistic or Animistic might fit, but labels were for gods and little children.

While completing the packing, I heard a light knock at the door, opened it, and Villiam stepped in as I was asking him, "How many people were praying for me?"

"Just one, me."

After we finished packing, we decided that we would need two taxis to transport the artifacts to the airport. Villiam made a phone call, and we soon met the drivers downstairs. I was relieved and was feeling perfectly normal, relaxed, and calm.

"Let's all go out for dinner before leaving for the airport." I offered. I felt I needed to show some extra appreciation for the drivers since they showed up so early.

After dining at a first class Brazilian restaurant, the four of us crammed the cargo into both taxis and headed for the airport. We were a curious site with nine-foot long blowguns sticking out the windows.

"Muito obrigdo!" I exclaimed while thanking the two drivers for their services and handing the young men a generous tip. "Bon dia."—A final farewell. It was 3 a.m., on day 30 of my trip.

The assorted cargo was perfectly packed. Several thousand dollars' worth of one-of-a-kind ethnographic jungle artifacts. Villiam helped me carry the load and present the materials to the government officials. No greater obstacles confronted a trader than government officials.

"Sorry," they said. "You may only check on the plane what you can carry to this desk by yourself."

I repeated, in a polite tone, "Are you stating that if I can get this load to the desk without any additional help moving it, you will accept the cargo?"

"Yes," they confirmed.

Villiam and I backed off and relocated the cargo to a spacious area out of the way of incoming passengers.

"Unpack everything," I said to Villiam. He gave me a puzzled look. No time to explain, we had to move fast.

Villiam began cutting up the six boxes as I emptied my exceptionally strong, expandable North Face backpack. I opened it to the max. Filling the pack with all the small items, cramming them into every square centimeter of the now five-foot pack. Two hundred and forty-five Ateori Indian arrows tipped with three to nine inch metal points were strapped to one side of the backpack, while nine Maku Indian blowguns were secured to the opposite side of the pack. We were ready. I was ready.

Confronting Customs

I was not sure customs was ready for this unusual check-in. I kept my fingers crossed. I was not allowed any assistance while lifting the heavy, burdensome load, undoubtedly weighing over 150 pounds. Two hours before, I could not have done it. Looking down at the mass, I knew that I had to get it to the desk. The clock was ticking. I squatted while using both my arms and legs, put one strap over my shoulder, eased up slowly, positioned my other arm through the opposite strap and stood up.

While doing so, I could hear the intro to 2001 Space Odyssey playing in my head, and without a doubt, I'm sure that I looked like something from outer space while walking carefully towards the officials. These were the days when government officials actually still had a sense of humor. Ordinarily phlegmatic and radiating a scowl of governmental power, these two Brazilian agents exploded with laughter and accepted my one-person cargo.

"Muito obrigado," I thanked Villiam for all that he had done, and said that I would see him the next year. I handed him a one hundred dollar bill, and boarded the plane for the states.

We were in the air for only a few minutes when I became aware of a rather strange coincidence. Two passengers sitting directly in front of me were Catholic priests. One was easily identifiable, donning his white collar, and the other was dressed in a business suit. At the time, I didn't think much about the coincidence; however, these two priests would play a very important role on my return trip.

With three seats to myself, I thought I could finally relax. I made it, I almost couldn't believe I survived the ordeal. Then it hit me hard, something was physically wrong with me. I had to urinate about every fifteen minutes, had difficulties focusing, and my hands were shaking.

"What in the hell is wrong," I thought. I was as sick as I had been in my room in Manaus and getting sicker. Lying down, I attempted to rest, but rest was impossible.

I tried to hold it together until we reached the states because I didn't want to ask anyone for help. In another hour, my rugged individualism would change.

"Excuse me sir, are you a priest?" I asked.

"Yes, we both are."

"I've got a serious problem."

"How can we help you sir?"

"Well," I paused, "I've been in the Amazon for thirty days, and during the last half of the trip I have gotten progressively sicker. I don't know if I can make it off this plane and check my cargo through US customs, and I have an extremely valuable assortment of Amazon artifacts–all legal, of course."

I verbally listed the various artifacts that they would see if they were willing to help. I continued as I was internally collapsing. "I have tickets for each bundle. Brazilian customs separated my one man carry-on entry into seven separate bundles."

The priests appeared puzzled, but made an honest effort to understand my strange situation. Their body language reflected that they were interested in possibly helping me if they could. I made it clear to them that I had made contact with the Yanomamö and that I had visited remote areas of the Amazon.

"I have attempted, for several days, to find out what is wrong with me but haven't had any luck." Shaking, I handed them my business card. They could see that I was legitimate.

"What would you like for us to do?" asked one of the priests.

"All you need to do is take these seven tickets and walk the cargo through customs. If they accept the shipment, they will send it to El Paso. If they do not, I will have to return to Florida. The priests agreed to help.

"Sign the labels, and we will do everything we can to help you."

I tried to sign the labels. Impossible. My hands were shaking so uncontrollably I could not connect my pen with the labels. As a last resort, I handed the priests my business card and requested that they complete the labeling. Thank god, they did. I passed out.

The Florida Hospital

The doctor looked down on me as I woke in the Florida hospital. He was wearing a reassuring smile on his face as he said, "You're going to be fine. The IVs are in your arms because you are extremely dehydrated. The priests called the hospital and provided us with some information regarding your trip. You have to rest here for two days before leaving for home. The medicine you took for giardia worked. The parasites are gone; however, all of those different types of medicines that you took while trying to kill the giardia produced a serious chemical reaction in your system. That's why you were shaking. You could have died, but all you need is rest and as much water as you can drink in order to rehydrate and flush your system of the remaining chemicals. You should be better in two days."

Walking quickly through the El Paso airport crowd, I headed straight to the baggage area. Lying on the floor was my entire cargo. The priests came through with flying colors. I checked in with customs, and while exiting the airport, I gave a backwards glance, watched passengers ride the escalator to the next floor, and in a flash of realization something profoundly unsettling yet liberating occurred to me: regardless of the mortal perils, the treacherous parasites, the blistering heat and drenching rains – I would return to the Amazon. Not now and not in a month, but soon. This place was calling out to me or perhaps it had become a part of me when I drank the water from its rivers – pulsating like the blood through my veins, the lush tropical landscape was a part of me now. For whatever reason we were now eternally bound.

Larry and Marilyn Baron buy, sell and trade for authentic and rare artifacts, traveling to exotic locales.

Photos by J.R. Hernandez, El Paso Times

INDIANA JONES OF EL PASO

Woulvaan Indian baskets caught Baron's eye on one of his thrilling trips.

INDIANA JONES
OF EL PASO

Woulvaan Indian baskets caught Baron's eye on one of his thrilling trips.

Store owner has risked life to get artifacts

By Matthew Aguilar
El Paso Times

Ten years ago, Larry Baron found himself sitting in a semi-circle with Yanomomo Indians in Brazil's Amazonas jungle watching nervously as the Indians took a hit of Ebene, a hallucinogen powder that is blown into their nostrils by a fellow Yanomomo.

He watched anxiously as the powder took effect, and the unpredictable Yanomomos began to make "contact" with the demons. Baron was educated enough in ancient Yanomomo culture to know what could be next: the dreaded "magical death."

Baron immediately realized that he would be the target of the ritual when an older Yanomomo, his face painted a grim white, called him out.

"Three times (a Yanomomo) came at me, hollering and screaming, putting his hands on my shoulders," Baron recalled. "He picked up a knife and tried to stab me, but I grabbed his wrist

Satere Indian masks are among the items for sale at LeBaron's Primitive Indian Artifacts at 500 N. Oregon.

and held tightly."

Finally, the two were separated, and Baron, trying hard not to show fear, realized he was far removed from the comparatively safe streets of El Paso.

"It scared me thoroughly," Baron said.

Baron, the owner of LeBaron's Primitive Indian Artifacts on 500 N. Oregon, has had to survive several harrowing experiences such as this one in order to bring back some of his shop's most impressive items.

He has traveled the world to get wood masks from Ghana, Africa; cow skulls from Mexico, Yanomomo bows and arrows from the Amazon and canoes from Panama. He has also traveled to Peru, Bolivia, England, Belgium, Belize, the Yukon, Guatemala, Honduras, Panama, El Salvador.

Please see **Artifacts** Page 5

About the Author

A native Texan, Larry Baron has traveled five continents for more than thirty years, collecting ethnographic materials from indigenous tribes. A trained anthropologist, Mr. Baron has traveled far up the Feeder Rivers of the Amazon, the deep reaches of Africa, and remote villages of Mexico and Central America, trading with rarely-visited tribes for artifacts that are common to them but rarely seen outside their environment.

At the age of fifteen, he found an eleven thousand year old pristine Clovis Point in the south plains of Texas while searching for artifacts following a sandstorm. Driven by a passionate interest in primitive cultures, Larry acquired his formal anthropological training, beginning as an exchange student at the University of the Americas in Cholula, Puebla, Mexico, and culminating with a B.A. in anthropology at Adams State College in Alamosa, Colorado. He earned his Master's degree in secondary education and administration from Steven F. Austin State University in Nacogdoches, Texas. Mr. Baron also earned an additional eighteen graduate hours in anthropology along with thousands of hours of field work while collecting artifacts from various countries.

In addition to his travels, Mr. Baron taught middle and high school for eight years. During this period, he initiated historical societies for students in many schools and produced numerous state and national history fair winners. He was awarded at least three outstanding teacher awards, including a special award from the Van Horn Historical Society. More recently, he taught an anthropology program for the University of Texas in El Paso. He has given numerous anthropological presentations for various colleges, universities, and museums.

To find out more information about Larry Baron, and to see various artifacts collected by him, please visit his website lebaronsprimitives.com

Made in the USA
Charleston, SC
23 April 2016